DEDICATION

To Doctor Ibram X Kendi. May you find the peace needed within yourself to stop dividing people into race-based moral categories before America cedes all the progress it's made in the last sixty years.

CONTENTS

Table of Contents

The Little Book of Woke Jokes

(jokes ruined by)

The Tired Moderate

INTRODUCTION

Sometimes you just can't be there. You want to be there - to monitor employee banter, to point out implicit biases on coffee shop menus, to berate and chastise bigots who think it's somehow permissible to interact with oppressed minorities when you're not on hand to supervise ...

The simple fact is you can't be everywhere. At the same time, the demand - nay, the *need* - for woke interventions has never been higher.

Enter *The Little Book of Woke Jokes*.

Now you can suck the joy out of exchanges you don't even know are happening. Just angrily heave *The Little Book of Woke Jokes* into a room, threaten reputational destruction if your coworkers, friends, or family members don't read it, and voilà! Progress!

Overachievers will probably want to follow up the lessons contained below with direct scoldings, and I enthusiastically support this. After all - if the unWoke don't take their medicine, they'll never get better.

TRAMPLING PUNCHLINES FOR JUSTICE

What does a nosy pepper do?

Excuse me, are you LatinX? If you aren't and you laugh at this, you're racist. Don't bother denying your racism either, racists always do that and it doesn't fool anybody.

(Gets jalapeño business!)

◆◆◆

Why are pirates called pirates?

Because white male oppressors wrote the history books and led a smear campaign against indigenous peoples just trying to survive their tyranny.

(Because they arrgh!)

◆◆◆

Why can't you explain puns to kleptomaniacs?

Kleptomania is a mental health issue, and the fact that you'd laugh at someone with a mental health issue tells me more about you than about them.

(They always take things literally.)

◆◆◆

How do you keep a bagel from getting away?

Unless you're literally Jewish, stop. Just stop. I don't care if Jewish people aren't offended. I am, on their behalf, and I'm telling you to stop now. If Jewish people wanted to be part of jokes, they'd get into comedy.

(Put lox on it.)

♦♦♦

What kind of exercises do lazy people do?

This is blatant body shaming. Every body is beautiful and every body is healthy. IT'S CALLED SCIENCE PEOPLE, MAYBE YOU'VE HEARD OF IT? Maybe instead of criticizing "lazy" people, try working on your unconscious biases.

(Diddly-squats.)

♦♦♦

How do we know that the ocean is friendly?

It doesn't rise up and murder us for abusing it with garbage, hunting its whales to extinction, spilling oil in it, or attacking it with nuclear bombs.

(It waves.)

♦♦♦

I waited all night to see where the sun would rise...

Oh goddess, is this another "it dawned on me" joke? Hey I've got one. Why did the straight white man tell a woman a joke? Because he's a vile pig only interested in sex.

(...And then it dawned on me.)

♦♦♦

Why did the frog take the bus to work today?

Because he lives in a disgusting capitalist society, where he'll get kicked to the street and starve to death if he doesn't waste his life in some soul-crushing, corporate job that only exists to make billionaires even richer while ruining the planet.

(His car got toad away.)

◆◆◆

Where does Batman go to the bathroom?

In whichever bathroom he/she/they chooses, you bigot.

(The batroom.)

◆◆◆

Why can't male ants sink?

(They're buoy-ant)

Um, excuse me, but "male" is a biological sex and "boy" is a gender, which is a social construct. I'm reporting you for hate speech.

◆◆◆

Why doesn't Dracula have any friends?

He's a rich white male who preys on women and the poor, so basically your typical beacon of white supremacy. You do the math.

(He's a real pain in the neck.)

◆◆◆

What do you call a boomerang that won't come back?

Maybe it was smart. Have you ever entertained the possibility that you're not worth coming back to? Try working on yourself.

(A stick.)

◆◆◆

What kind of water can't freeze?

Water subjected to the gradual warming of the planet because human activity is raising the level of carbon dioxide in our atmosphere.

(Hot water.)

◆◆◆

What did the pirate say when he turned 80?

He thanked all the shareholders and stepped down as CEO so he could spend more time playing golf on land STOLEN FROM INDIGENOUS PEOPLE all around the world.

(Aye matey.)

◆◆◆

Why was the baby strawberry crying?

It wanted us to stop dropping poison on it and go organic.

(Because her mom and dad were in a jam.)

◆◆◆

What did the buffalo say when his son left for college?

No means no, and if she's drunk, that means no, even if you're drunk too, and she started it. Also hesitation before yes means no because she might feel pressured. A retroactive no means no too. Anything less than an enthusiastic yes means no, and then it might be the result of social pressure, so assume it's still no. Just, no.

(Bison.)

♦♦♦

What do you call a fake noodle?

Oh right, because nobody but Italians can possibly know how to cook noodles. They're called Asians, not that our Eurocentric educational system cares enough to teach us about half the world's people.

(An impasta.)

♦♦♦

What did the 0 say to the 8?

It pointed out the systemic racism of math, despite the west culturally appropriating ARABIC numerals. Is there nothing white people can't ruin?

(Nice belt!)

♦♦♦

What do you call a pony with a cough?

Oppressed by a culture that sees a beautiful, wild animal and instinctively seeks to dominate and humiliate it by riding on top of it for pleasure.

(A little horse.)

♦♦♦

What did the shark say when he ate the clownfish?

I can feel the plastic worming its way through my system because Americans are too spoiled and self indulgent to stop using single-use plastic bags and then throwing them directly into my backyard.

(This tastes a little funny.)

What's orange and sounds like a carrot?

Jordan Peterson's followers are basically vegetables, so if you smeared them all with Agent Orange it would make them look like a carrot. They'd still sound like transphobes, but it wouldn't matter because they'd be dead soon.

(A parrot.)

♦♦♦

Why can't you hear a pterodactyl go to the bathroom?

They were all killed off by a giant asteroid, which is what should happen to humans. We're basically parasites sucking the life from the Earth. Everyone is stupid.

(Because the "P" is silent.)

♦♦♦

What does Charles Dickens keep in his spice rack?

White male privilege.

(The best of thymes, the worst of thymes.)

♦♦♦

Why should the number 288 never be mentioned?

Maybe because it's 287 more than the number of Black Presidents the United States has ever elected? It's also 288 more than the number of female Presidents. Keep that in mind when you're complaining about people being mean to you online.

(It's two gross.)

♦♦♦

What did the Tin Man say when he got run over by a steamroller?

He probably made a predictable, misogynistic remark about women drivers, ignoring the statistics about male drivers dying younger because MEN ARE IDIOTS.

("Curses! Foil again!")

◆◆◆

What did the bald man exclaim when he received a comb for a present?

He diminished the struggles People of Color face every day in the face of white supremacist America by complaining about not needing it because he's bald.

(Thanks— I'll never part with it!)

◆◆◆

What rhymes with orange?

Um, how about the colonialist history of oranges, that were planted by white Europeans in strategic places throughout the world so they could pick them to avoid scurvy on the long voyages they took to murder and oppress People of Color.

(No it doesn't.)

◆◆◆

What did the left eye say to the right eye?

My left eye sees white supremacy everywhere, so this hypothetical left eye of yours probably said, "hey, look at the pervasive racism in America."

(Between you and me, something smells.)

◆◆◆

Why don't Calculus majors throw house parties?

Because no one wants to go to a party with a bunch of white male incels who probably support rape culture because they can't get a woman to have sex with them. That's obviously why there are so few female mathematicians. Educate yourself.

(Because you should never drink and derive.)

◆◆◆

A man tells his doctor, "Doc, help me. I'm addicted to Twitter!"

Oh great, another "antiwoke" white man complaining about Twitter. Stop whining, your feelings don't matter. Way to make it all about you again, tool.

(The doctor replies, "Sorry, I don't follow you…")

◆◆◆

What's the best thing about Switzerland?

Not the fact that many Swiss used to fight as mercenaries for colonial European powers, murdering People of Color for money.

(I don't know, but the flag is a big plus.)

◆◆◆

Did you hear about the mathematician who's afraid of negative numbers?

Mathematicians are almost exclusively male due to a toxic culture that makes women feel unwelcome. I don't care what they're afraid of, besides equity.

(He'll stop at nothing to avoid them.)

Why do we tell actors to "break a leg?"

That's incredibly ableist. Did you even stop to think how that joke might make someone in a wheelchair feel?

(Because every play has a cast.)

◆◆◆

How many times can you subtract 10 from 100?

I bet if you subtracted 1 from 100 for every Person of Color arrested by racist police officers, you would hit 0 every day in America.

(Once. The next time you would be subtracting 10 from 90.)

◆◆◆

Knock! Knock!

Oh I get it, we're going to pretend to do a no-knock raid. Just pretend to shoot me already, I have a slam poetry reading to get to.

(Q: Who's there?
A: Control Freak.
Q: Con...
A: Okay, now you say, "Control Freak who?")

◆◆◆

Hear about the new restaurant called Karma?

No, but I'll send every cis white man I see there so he can be stripped of his white male privilege.

(There's no menu: You get what you deserve.)

◆◆◆

Did you hear about the actor who fell through the floorboards?

No, but if it was a man he was being paid twice as much as the woman next to him so I don't feel bad about it.

(He was just going through a stage.)

◆◆◆

Did you hear about the claustrophobic astronaut?

Unless the astronaut was a woman, I don't want to hear any boo-hoo stories about how hard his life is.

(He just needed a little space.)

◆◆◆

Why don't scientists trust atoms?

They're named after a man, because of the systemic exclusion of women in STEM fields.

(Because they make up everything.)

◆◆◆

Why did the chicken go to the séance?

To escape factory farming, a major contributor to climate change and antibiotic resistance, not to mention an inhumane way to treat animals. You should eat soy-based meat substitutes.

(To get to the other side.)

◆◆◆

Where are average things manufactured?

Meritocracy is racist, sexist, ableist, and heteronormative, because it amplifies existing power structures. Anyone who isn't a straight, white, cisgendered man is considered average by our white supremacist culture.

(The satisfactory.)

◆◆◆

How do you drown a hipster?

I can't believe you'd sit here and listen to yet another white man (it's always a white man) advocate violence. Disgusting.

(Throw him in the mainstream.)

◆◆◆

What sits at the bottom of the sea and twitches?

Um, the corpses of all the people the patriarchy has destroyed over the centuries? Billions of plankton who died because the fossil fuel industry bribed corrupt politicians to subsidize them and cut regulation? You tell me, Hitler.

(A nervous wreck.)

◆◆◆

Why did the yogurt go to the art exhibition?

To see all the ancient Middle Eastern artifacts that white European men STOLE from the indigenous populations.

(Because it was cultured.)

◆◆◆

What do you call an apology written in dots and dashes?

An admission of guilt to be used against whoever issued it. It should be translated into readable English - not "standard" English, which is a racist concept - and sent to the guilty person's employer, as well as being sprayed across social media to shame them.

(Re-Morse code.)

♦♦♦

Why did the hipster burn his mouth?

To atone for his white privilege.

(He drank the coffee before it was cool.)

♦♦♦

Did you hear about the two people who stole a calendar?

If it was a solar calendar then they deserve a medal. Lunar calendars are more accurate, easier to use, and more sensitive to cultural differences, which is why they were demonized and abolished by the white patriarchy.

(They each got six months.)

♦♦♦

How do poets say hello?

With a superior linguistic intensity the uneducated masses will never understand or appreciate because all they care about is fast food and sitcoms.

(Hey, haven't we metaphor?)

♦♦♦

Why did the Oreo go to the dentist?

I refuse to participate in any joke using a racist slur not aimed at white people. If I catch anyone using the "O word" around me I'm immediately whipping my phone out to record the confrontation we're going to have, so I can post it everywhere and send it to your manager.

(Because he lost his filling.)

◆◆◆

What do you get from a pampered cow?

Um, death, for you and the cow, which you've forced into servitude and misery because you can't be bothered to accept a vegan lifestyle. Vegans are SCIENTIFICALLY PROVEN to be happier, healthier, live longer, and be smarter than their murderous, speciest counterparts.

(Spoiled milk.)

◆◆◆

Why is it annoying to eat next to basketball players?

Because you're racist trash.

(They dribble all the time.)

◆◆◆

What breed of dog can jump higher than buildings?

Animals aren't here for your entertainment. How would you like it if someone forced you to do stupid tricks for food, then yelled at you if you didn't do them well enough?

(Any dog, because buildings can't jump.)

◆◆◆

Why did the M&M go to school?

To get out of its abusive home, enabled by "good" people who choose not to look at social inequities that contribute to problems like single parent households, and abusers.

(It wanted to be a Smartie.)

♦♦♦

What did the cop say to his belly button?

Probably nothing, he just opened fire. Unless the belly button was a WHITE MALE, then it was a long, friendly chat before politely escorting him to jail for MURDER.

(You're under a vest.)

♦♦♦

Why aren't koalas actual bears?

Stop stripping people's identities! It doesn't matter if they're not people, you need to stop creating hierarchies based on immutable characteristics. Nobody owes you a reason for their existence, especially if you're a white man.

(They don't meet the koalafications.)

♦♦♦

What do you call a rooster staring at a pile of lettuce?

A prisoner of the farm industrial complex.

(A chicken sees a salad.)

♦♦♦

Why did the nurse need a red pen at work?

To draw an X on all the privileged white men who refused to wear a mask to protect low-income frontline workers from Covid 19 because "DERP DERP DERP MAH FREEDUM."

(In case she needed to draw blood.)

◆◆◆

How do you throw a space party?

You fly into outer space and then throw a party. Did you just assume I wouldn't understand basic science because I'm a woman? If I'd been filming you I would have already put you on blast.

(You planet.)

◆◆◆

What do you call a train carrying bubblegum?

A symbol of imperialism and genocide against the Native American peoples. And gum.

(A chew-chew train.)

◆◆◆

Why did the math textbook visit the guidance counselor

So the guidance counselor could educate it on systemic racism and how it manifests itself in math, as described by the "shutdown stem" movement.

(It needed help figuring out its problems.)

◆◆◆

What did one ocean say to the other ocean?

Are you choking out all life inside of you because of acidification due to climate change? Are you as mad at baby boomers as I am?

(Nothing, it just waved.)

◆◆◆

Do you want to hear a construction joke?

No, I DON'T want to hear a joke set in a misogynistic environment famous for cat-calling and harassing women.

(Sorry, I'm still working on it.)

◆ ◆ ◆

Did you hear about the fire at the circus?

The word "circus" offends me. They're hives of animal abuse, not to mention the exploitation of little people, and self-identifying women with beards. All circuses need to close. NOW.

(It was in tents!)

◆ ◆ ◆

Why do ducks have feathers?

To repel oil every time a multi-national corporation decides quarterly profits and "shareholder value" mean more than leaving a functioning planet for our kids.

(To cover their butt quacks!)

◆ ◆ ◆

What's the difference between a hippo and a zippo?

Nothing, both are perfect the way they are, and fat shaming is disgusting. Did you know that women considered "overweight" in America today used to be the most attractive? It's all cultural programming. Think about that next time you feel like crapping on someone just because you don't think they're "hot" enough.

(One is really heavy and the other's a little lighter.)

◆ ◆ ◆

When does a joke become a 'dad' joke?

When it's already been told so many times by women that men start to understand it.

(When it becomes apparent.)

♦♦♦

Why did the bullet lose his job?

Because he ended up in another unarmed Person of Color.

(He got fired.)

♦♦♦

How do you measure a snake?

By the number of ignorant people trying to kill it because they're too stupid to know which ones are dangerous. EDUCATE YOURSELF PEOPLE.

(In inches—they don't have feet.)

♦♦♦

Where does a waitress with only one leg work?

Multiple places, because the gender pay gap guarantees she'll need to.

(IHOP.)

♦♦♦

What does a house wear?

It depends if it's somewhere white people feel like living, then it would wear the brand of gentrification, racism, and theft.

(Address!)

♦♦♦

Two windmills are standing on a wind farm. One asks, 'What's your favorite kind of music?'

The death throes of the fossil fuel industry.

(The other replies, 'I'm a big metal fan.')

♦♦♦

The first rule of the Alzheimer's club is...

Oh Emm Gee, you are so ableist I'm literally queasy right now. How would YOU like it if you had a severe degenerative disease and someone turned you into a punchline? Huh? Pig.

(Wait, where are we again?)

♦♦♦

Why were they called the "dark ages?"

Because our white supremacist culture describes anything it doesn't like as non-white. I've started a petition on change.org to force schools to stop using racist terms like this.

(Because there were a lot of knights.)

♦♦♦

Want to hear a joke about a roof?

Is it about the housing crisis in most major cities, and how anyone opposing rent control is a heartless Nazi?

(The first one's on the house.)

♦♦♦

Why do teddy bears never want to eat anything?

Because they've been fat shamed by the patriarchy into thinking anorexia is sexy, and that being sexy is the primary purpose of women.

(Because they're always stuffed.)

◆◆◆

Did you hear about the cheese factory that exploded in France?

Don't you dare make this about Islam, DON'T YOU DARE.

(There was nothing left but de Brie.)

◆◆◆

Where should you go in the room if you're feeling cold?

To the warm embrace of the socialist left, and away from the icy claws of the capitalist, murderous right.

(The corner—they're usually 90 degrees.)

◆◆◆

What's the difference between a poorly-dressed man on a unicycle and a well-dressed man on a bicycle?

Levels of oppression.

(Attire.)

◆◆◆

You know why you never see elephants hiding up in trees?

Because humans keep destroying their natural habitats and poaching them, so there aren't many left.

(Because they're really good at it.)

◆◆◆

What's the difference between an oral thermometer and a rectal thermometer?

This sounds homophobic and sex negative. I'm recording you right now, just so you know.

(The taste, mostly.)

◆◆◆

I told my friend ten jokes to make him laugh.

Because that's the role of women, right? To make men laugh? We're not human beings with needs or dreams of our own, we're just here to "make him laugh." You make me sick.

(Sadly, no pun in ten did.)

◆◆◆

I couldn't believe the highway department called my dad a thief.

They were probably right. Just check any British museum and you'll find all the evidence you'll ever need of imperialism and theft committed by men just like your dad. All men should be in jail.

(But when I got home, the signs were all there.)

◆◆◆

Why did the cowboy get a wiener dog?

To help him better commit genocide against Native Americans, who still suffer in white supremacist America. Sorry, but you don't get a pass for having a cute dog.

(He wanted to get a long little doggie.)

◆◆◆

Did you hear about the painter who was hospitalized?

It was probably poverty-based malnutrition after the millionth subhuman tried to pay her with "recognition."

(The doctors say it was due to too many strokes.)

◆◆◆

What do you call a cow with a twitch?

A victim of the meat eating patriarchy.

(Beef jerky.)

◆◆◆

I started a new job as a tailor last week.

I'm sorry your job is being outsourced to a country with no labor regulations where children or women will do it for starvation wages so some multinational corporation can increase its dividend.

(It's been sew-sew.)

◆◆◆

My wife accused me the other day of being too immature.

She was probably right. Men are gigantic babies that require wives in order to function at a basic level, let alone raise a child.

(I told her there were no girls allowed in my fort.)

◆◆◆

Someone stole my mood ring yesterday.

Probably because all the wealth in America is concentrated in the top 1%, and the rest of us are left to fight each other for scraps.

(I still don't know how I feel about that.)

◆◆◆

I tried to catch fog yesterday.

You won't have fog left soon, because human activity is heating the planet and destroying weather as we know it.

(Mist.)

◆◆◆

Someone stole my Microsoft Office and they're gonna pay.

I'm sorry, are we supposed to care about stealing from a giant monopoly started by yet another straight, white, cisgendered man? Where were you when they were stealing Palestine? Racist.

(You have my Word.)

◆◆◆

What do you call a dog with no legs?

Abuse of animals is an early warning sign that you're a serial killer. This joke is not a joke.

(It doesn't matter, it's not going to come anyway.)

◆◆◆

I got a new job last week as the new top dog at Old MacDonald's farm.

They needed another person to violently cram as many chickens as possible into the tiny room where they'll lay eggs until we kill them.

(I'm the new C-I-E-I-O.)

◆◆◆

Why are frogs always so happy?

They don't live near people.

(They eat whatever bugs them.)

◆◆◆

Whenever you jump on a trampoline, did you know it changes the season?

What's the difference, now that we're heating the planet to the point that entire ecosystems are collapsing?

(No matter what time of year, it always becomes spring time.)

◆◆◆

What do you call a musician with problems?

A musician. Stop demonizing mental health issues, it's ableist, and makes YOU the problem.

(A trebled man.)

◆◆◆

What do you call a religious person who sleepwalks?

They ALL sleepwalk, that's why they're religious and not woke.

(A roamin' Catholic.)

◆◆◆

Did you hear about the carrot detective?

If you hear the word "detective" and envision a man, you're a sexist piece of crap.

(He always got to the root of every case.)

◆◆◆

What washes up on very small beaches?

Plastic, styrofoam, and other garbage we still haven't found the will to BAN because greedy corporations lobby our corrupt politicians so they can maximize quarterly profits. Who needs a planet anyway, right?

(Micro-waves)

◆◆◆

What did one elevator say to the other?

Wouldn't it be nice if these exploitative humans could use the stairs instead of burning COAL AND OIL to make us lift them up and down?

(I think I'm coming down with something.)

◆◆◆

Why did the tomato turn red?

Someone genetically modified it to look "prettier" instead of being healthy, because that's what our stupid culture values.

(It saw the salad dressing.)

◆◆◆

Why won't skeletons fight each other?

They forgot the patriarchy's cultural indoctrination that tells us we have to fight each other instead of banding together to overthrow the real oppressors.

(They just don't have the guts.)

♦♦♦

What time is it when the clock strikes 13?

Time to fight systemic racism and white supremacy in America.

(Time to get a new clock.)

♦♦♦

Why did the kid bring a ladder to school?

So she could break through the glass ceiling imposed by American's racist, heteronormative patriarchy.

(Because she wanted to go to high school.)

♦♦♦

Where would you find an elephant?

In the wilds of India or Africa if you're a human being, in a zoo if you're HITLER.

(The same place you lost her.)

♦♦♦

What building in your town has the most stories?

The Police Station, and the stories are all about racial inequities and injustice.

(The public library.)

What's worse than finding a worm in your apple?

White supremacy, and its enablers, also known as Republicans.

(Finding half a worm.)

♦♦♦

What is a computer's favorite snack?

Our personal information, served to corporations for the enrichment of a handful of tech bros and their financial backers because our government is too corrupt to stand up to them.

(Computer chips.)

♦♦♦

What animal is always at a baseball game?

A lazy husband with a lonely, unappreciated wife at home.

(A bat.)

♦♦♦

Why did the kid cross the playground?

To escape the school shooter who couldn't get the mental help he needed because of our corrupt, for-profit health care system, but could get an AK-47 because we're too stupid to ban machine guns.

(To get to the other slide.)

♦♦♦

Why did the cookie go to the hospital?

To kill more people with the chemicals that profit-obsessed mega corporations put in refined foods.

(Because he felt crummy.)

♦ ♦ ♦

What did the little corn say to the mama corn?

Why is the government subsidizing me for ethanol when renewables are obviously the way to fight climate change? Is it because our first election primaries in every Presidential election are held in farming states who want subsidies?

(Where is pop corn?)

♦ ♦ ♦

What kind of tree fits in your hand?

The remnants of the Amazon rain forest after Brazil's right-wing government finishes destroying it.

(A palm tree.)

♦ ♦ ♦

What has ears but cannot hear?

Republicans.

(A cornfield.)

♦ ♦ ♦

What did one plate say to the other plate?

I hope they don't POISON us with non-organic food again. They must not care about the Earth AT ALL.

(Dinner is on me.)

Why did the student eat his homework?

His graduate school stipend was so pathetic that he was starving, even though he was doing the bulk of the teaching.

(Because the teacher told him it was a piece of cake.)

♦♦♦

What is brown, hairy and wears sunglasses?

ENOUGH RACIST JOKES. Consider yourself reported, and if I can find out where you live, I'm totally doxxing you.

(A coconut on vacation.)

♦♦♦

What do you say to a rabbit on its birthday?

Congratulations, I hope some dumb suburban mom doesn't buy you as a gift for her resource-guzzling child, then dump you outside when you stop being cute and new.

(Hoppy Birthday.)

♦♦♦

What's the one thing will you get every year on your birthday, guaranteed?

Warmer summers.

(A year older.)

♦♦♦

Why do candles always go on the top of cakes?

Because rich white men decided a long time ago that that's the way we should ALL celebrate, and why on earth would we ever question the wisdom of rich white men?

(Because it's hard to light them from the bottom.)

◆◆◆

What goes up but never comes down?

The level of fragility in white people.

(Your age.)

◆◆◆

What does every birthday end with?

A middle finger to Donald Trump.

(The letter Y.)

◆◆◆

Why did the little girl hit her birthday cake with a hammer?

She was sick of the gender pay gap being justified by Jordan Peterson fans and it's illegal to hit them with the hammer. For now.

(It was a pound cake.)

◆◆◆

Why was the equal sign so humble?

Because it knows equality is a racist goal. Only equity will do, and if we don't get it, we'll tear everything down.

(Because he wasn't greater than or less than anyone else.)

◆◆◆

What do you call guys who love math?

Sexist.

(Algebros.)

◆◆◆

Why was the fraction nervous about marrying the decimal?

Because marriage is an oppressive tool of the patriarchy designed to trade and hold women like property.

(Because he would have to convert.)

◆◆◆

Why was the math book sad?

Because it represented systemic racism and whiteness.

(Because it had too many problems.)

◆◆◆

Why does nobody talk to circles?

The same reason nobody talks to white people - it's useless and exhausting.

(Because there's no point.)

◆◆◆

What do you call a sleeping bull?

A feminist you haven't made angry enough to act yet.

(A bull-dozer.)

♦♦♦

How do you fit more pigs on a farm?

Cram them in with violent force, then write laws making it illegal for journalists to record what happens on a factory farm. We'll all just sit here getting sicker so the real pigs can gorge themselves on animal flesh and money.

(Build a sty-scraper.)

♦♦♦

How did the pirate get his flag so cheaply?

It was made in a sweatshop by a multi-national conglomerate that barely pretends to care about human rights. Thanks globalization!

(He bought it on sail.)

♦♦♦

How do pirates know that they are pirates?

They're labeled at birth by bigoted doctors who cling to the outdated belief that pirateness is not fluid.

(They think, therefore they arrr.)

♦♦♦

Why do melons have weddings?

Why does anyone? It's just a way for a man to stamp his badge of ownership on a woman and turn her into a breeder. The whole institution should be outlawed.

(Because they cantaloupe.)

Do I enjoy making courthouse puns?

If your white privilege means you're blind to the systemic racism in our courts, then yes, yes you do. Otherwise you wouldn't joke about something this deadly serious.

(Guilty.)

♦♦♦

What starts with an "O", ends with "nions" and can make you cry?

Listening to stupid racists explain why they voted for Donald Trump. Oh wait, I was supposed to start with the letter "O." Whatever. Sorry, not sorry.

(Opinions.)

♦♦♦

How do you make holy water?

Get a bunch of intolerant hypocrites to say it's "holy," but only in the oppressive, Judeo-Christian sense of the word.

(You boil the hell out of it.)

♦♦♦

What do you call someone with no body and no nose?

A victim. Have some respect and stop punching down, you foul excuse for a human being.

(Nobody knows.)

♦♦♦

What sound does a witch's car make?

The same as everyone else's. Wicca is an ancient and noble belief system that teaches us to be one with Mother Earth, so it's no surprise the violent, patriarchal Judeo-Christian power structure continues to tear it down.

(Broom broom!)

♦♦♦

Why doesn't saying "no" to drugs work?

Because the drug war was never meant to stop drugs from killing minorities, it was meant to destabilize Latin American governments so our imperialist foreign policy could continue to benefit the ultra-wealthy.

(Because if I'm talking to my drugs, I probably already said yes.)

♦♦♦

What did the duck say when she bought lipstick?

"She" should have said, "I refuse to reinforce gender conforming stereotypes created and upheld by men for their own sexual gratification."

(Put it on my bill!)

♦♦♦

What do you call a man with a rubber toe?

Handy-abled. Oh my goddess, check your privilege.

(Roberto!)

♦♦♦

What do you give to a sick lemon?

Chronic illness is a feature of everyday life for millions of Americans, particularly People of Color, who are disproportionately impoverished and face systemic discrimination in the health care system. This isn't funny.

(Lemon aid)

◆◆◆

What did the janitor say when he jumped out of the closet?

"Give me a livable wage you white oppressor!" Hah! Get it? It's funny because you're evil.

("Supplies!")

◆◆◆

Why don't ants get sick?

Because they don't have a greedy health care system more interested in shareholder profits than making people healthy.

(They have anty-bodies.)

◆◆◆

What do you call someone who immigrated to Sweden?

How about "refugee?" Have you stopped to consider how American foreign policy is driving millions of people into Europe from Africa? Or how immigration from Latin America is often a response to violence perpetuated in the name of America's "drug war?" Prick.

(Artificial Swedener)

◆◆◆

What's the dumbest animal in the jungle?

Humans. They're the only animal willing to DESTROY their habitat for short-term gain.

(A polar bear!)

◆◆◆

What's the most terrifying word in nuclear physics?

"Clean energy." I don't care if it's two words, solar panels don't create toxic waste by the ton and occasionally explode. Educate yourself.

("Oops!")

◆◆◆

What did Mario say when he broke up with Princess Peach?

Who? And what makes you think he initiated the break up? She was probably sick of his toxic, macho attitude and ghosted him. Now he's "dumping" her to save face.

("It's not you, it's a-me, Mario!")

Holiday Bonus!

Why didn't the skeleton go to school?

She didn't have the stomach for another lecture on how great Christopher Columbus was, or any of the other genocidal white men the repressive educational system forces children to worship.

(His heart wasn't in it.)

♦♦♦

What monster plays tricks on Halloween?

The moderate Democrat that says he'll vote for the Equal Rights Amendment.

(Prank-enstein.)

♦♦♦

What does a witch use to do her hair?

Something deliberately overpriced. Heard of the "pink tax?" Yeah, I didn't think so. Women pay more than men for everything, and we're paid less. But please, continue with your puerile joke.

(Scarespray.)

◆◆◆

What room does a ghost not need?

A retirement room since no one born after 1990 in America will ever retire.
Thanks baby boomers!

(A living room.)

◆◆◆

Are black cats bad luck?

No, this is just another racist trope. That you'd even ask that is disgusting.
You're why we can't have nice things.

(Sure, if you're a mouse.)

◆◆◆

When is it bad luck to be followed by a black cat?

Again with the racism. You think we can't tell that you mean "black man"
here? Cancelled!

(When you're a mouse.)

◆◆◆

What do you call two witches living together?

A happy couple, you Christian homophobe.

(Broommates.)

◆◆◆

What's big, scary and has three wheels?

An mildly disappointed white man with a bunch of guns. And three wheels.

(A monster on a tricycle.)

♦♦♦

Why don't vampires have more friends?

Because they suck the life from everything around them, leaving death and carnage in their wake for their own benefit. Oh wait, those are banks.

(Because they are a pain in the neck.)

♦♦♦

What do you call a witch who goes to the beach?

For Gaia's sake! LEAVE. WOMEN. ALONE. Don't call them anything! Don't talk to them at all! And if you tell them to smile I swear I'm going to vomit all over you.

(A sand-witch.)

♦♦♦

What kinds of pants do ghosts wear?

Whatever's comfortable. Stop policing fashion, we're not here to turn you on. Jackass.

(Boo-jeans.)

♦♦♦

How does a snowman lose weight?

It's snowPERSON. And she doesn't, she's fine the way she is and doesn't care about your ableist, arbitrary standards of beauty.

(He waits for the weather to get warmer.)

◆◆◆

What did one snowman say to the other snowman?

SNOWPERSON. Also, "maybe we should betray our white solidarity
and stand for progress."

(Do you smell carrots?)

◆◆◆

Who isn't hungry at Thanksgiving?

Wall Street fat cats already gorged on profits from outsourcing jobs to
countries with no labor laws.

(The turkey—he's already stuffed.)

◆◆◆

What's the key to a great Thanksgiving dinner?

Feigning gratitude to the butchers that founded America on the back on
indigenous peoples, then shouting at your uncle for being racist before he
even has a chance to spew any of his gross Republican talking points.

(The tur-key.)

◆◆◆

Why did pilgrims' pants always fall down?

Because the Native Americans didn't have belts to steal before the
pilgrims MURDERED them.

(Because they wore their belt buckle on their hat.)

◆◆◆

What's the best dance to do on Thanksgiving?

Whatever dance can undo centuries of tragedy spawned by white settlers destroying every culture they come in contact with.

(The turkey trot.)

♦♦♦

What do elves learn in school?

If they go to school in a systemically racist town, they learn Santa Claus is white.

(The elf-abet.)

♦♦♦

Why did the Pilgrims sail from England to America?

They were bored with raping and murdering French people.

(Because they missed their plane.)

♦♦♦

When the Pilgrims landed, where did they stand?

On land they were about to steal.

(On their feet.)

♦♦♦

Why did the police arrest the turkey?

They were white and it wasn't.

(They suspected it of fowl play.)

♦♦♦

What should you wear to Thanksgiving dinner?

Your guilt and shame at the genocidal American heritage.

(A har-vest.)

◆◆◆

If the Pilgrims were alive today, what would they be most famous for?

War crimes.

(Their age.)

◆◆◆

What kind of music did Pilgrims listen to?

The death cries of those who helped them.

(Plymouth Rock.)

◆◆◆

What smells the best at a Thanksgiving dinner?

The blood of oppressors.

(Your nose.)

◆◆◆

Why does Santa work at the North Pole?

Republicans gave him a tax break and let him classify the elves as "contractors" so he didn't have to give them benefits. Enjoy all your cheap toys. Cretins.

(Because the penguins kicked him out of the South Pole.)

◆◆◆

How does a sheep say Merry Christmas?

Happy Holidays, because even sheep aren't arrogant enough to disregard minority beliefs.

(Fleece Navidad.)

◆◆◆

What is an elf's favorite kind of music?

(Wrap music.)

Other people's cultures aren't your punchlines. Never mention rap, hip-hop, jazz, or any other music from under represented cultures again unless it's to apologize for appropriating them.

◆◆◆

Why did Rudolph get a bad grade on his report card?

His teacher was speciest.

(Because he went down in history.)

◆◆◆

What do you get when you combine a Christmas tree with a computer?

A consumer society that can ruin the earth without getting off the couch.

(A pine-apple.)

◆◆◆

Why are Christmas trees bad at sewing?

They're not, they just don't work for starvation wages like toy making corporations demand.

(Because they always drop their needles.)

◆◆◆

Why was the Easter Bunny so upset?

He's a manifestation of the Christian theft of indigenous holidays, thinly coated with whatever local customs the patriarchy thought might help it retain control over the population it was oppressing at the moment.

(He was having a bad hare day.)

◆◆◆

How does the Easter bunny stay in shape?

Running from meat eating murderers.

(Lots of eggs-ercise.)

◆◆◆

What do you call a bunny who isn't smart?

How elitist are these jokes going to get? Now rabbits have to be smart enough for you? This is such a pompous joke, I just can't even.

(A hare brain.)

◆◆◆

What happened when the Easter Bunny met the rabbit of his dreams?

They gay married and rode off into the sunset. Homophobe.

(They lived hoppily ever after.)

◆◆◆

Why shouldn't you tell an Easter egg a good joke?

Because you should have the courtesy to let the rabbit hatch before you start man-splaining the world to it, or accosting it with your dumb dad jokes.

(It might crack up.)

◆◆◆

What did one colored egg say to the other?

Oh. My. Goddess. I can't believe you used that word. I'm screenshotting this. You're getting dragged on Twitter for sure. Racist.

(Heard any good yolks lately?)

QUICK QUIPS
(AND WHY THEY'RE PROBLEMATIC)

Helvetica and Times New Roman walk into a bar. "Get out of here!" shouts the bartender. "We don't serve your type."

This joke has clear Jim Crow overtones, and it's unbelievable someone in the 21st century would tell it.

♦♦♦

Yesterday I saw a guy spill all his Scrabble letters on the road. I asked him, "What's the word on the street?"

If the guy spilling the letters in the street was a Person of Color, some white woman named "Karen" would have called the police on him, and they probably would have shot him.

♦♦♦

A woman in labour suddenly shouted, "Shouldn't! Wouldn't! Couldn't! Didn't! Can't!" "Don't worry," said the doctor. "Those are just contractions."

First of all, the word "woman" is non-inclusive. Men can give birth too, so we say "birthers" now. Second, I need to know the racial background of both people in this joke. Third, enforcing arbitrary grammar rules is a method of suppression use by the oppressor class.

◆◆◆

A bear walks into a bar and says, "Give me a whiskey... and a cola." "Why the big pause?" asks the bartender. The bear shrugged. "I'm not sure. I was born with them."

Every year thousands of wild animals are shot because they wander into neighborhoods that HUMANS built in what used to be the animals' habitat. Humans are the real pandemic on this planet.

◆◆◆

I told my wife she was drawing her eyebrows too high. She looked at me surprised.

She shouldn't have, since men have spent centuries criticizing women for their makeup, then complaining when they don't wear any.

◆◆◆

Time flies like an arrow... Fruit flies like a banana.

Haha funny. Not so funny is the intensive genetic modification bananas have suffered to get to the pretty yellow color that Americans demand before they'll eat fruit instead of planet-murdering, factory farmed hamburgers.

◆◆◆

I got my daughter a fridge for her birthday. I can't wait to see her face light up when she opens it.

Why? So she can cook for you? You do know women make up more than half of college graduates in America now, right? Troglodyte.

◆◆◆

19 and 20 got into a fight. 21.

Har har. Not even numbers are safe from patriarchal violence. At least no angry incel brought an AR-15 to the fight and shot all the teens.

◆◆◆

There's a fine line between a numerator and a denominator... Only a fraction of people will get this joke.

"Fraction" is code for "men." Only men will get this joke? This is classic systemic sexism. If you laughed at it, you're part of the problem.

◆◆◆

My teachers told me I'd never amount to much since I procrastinate so much. I told them, "Just you wait!"

Those "teachers" sound like they were there to prep you for a life of servitude to the exploitative capitalist system. Maybe if THEY worked harder at not being fascists, THEY would amount to something.

◆◆◆

I took the shell off of my racing snail, thinking it would make him faster. But if anything, it made him more sluggish.

Just another example of humans ruining the natural world for their own amusement. I hope you're proud of yourself.

◆◆◆

A Roman legionnaire walks into a bar, holds up two fingers and says, "Five beers, please."

And if the bartender doesn't understand Roman numerals, the legionnaire stabs him. Because Romans were the original white imperialists, exporting their fascism as far as their butchery would allow.

◆◆◆

How do you get a squirrel to like you? Act like a nut.

Is that supposed to be funny? Making fun of the mentally ill is disgusting and I hope everyone sees what a piece of trash you are.

◆◆◆

When a woman is giving birth, she is literally kidding.

Seriously? Are you seriously so stuck in the 1950s that you believe only women give birth? This is so transphobic it makes me sick.

◆◆◆

I sold my vacuum cleaner; it was just gathering dust.

It's well documented that women, despite participating in the work force, continue to do most of the housework while men loaf on the couch and watch sports. So maybe instead of selling the vacuum cleaner you should try using it. Useless man baby.

◆◆◆

I threw a boomerang a few years ago. I now live in constant fear.

Maybe you should have gone and fetched your stupid toy. It's probably rotting in a land fill right now while you sit here making dumb jokes.

◆◆◆

You don't need a parachute to go skydiving, you need a parachute to go skydiving a second time.

Oh right, let's make fun of suicide, because everyone's supposed to come out of their birthing human (don't you DARE say "mother") perfect, and we should just abandon anyone who doesn't.

♦♦♦

Do you remember that joke I told you about my spine? It was about a weak back!

Millions of people suffer from Scoliosis, and I hardly think they'd appreciate this joke.

♦♦♦

My favorite word is "drool." It just rolls off the tongue.

This is exactly the kind of insensitivity I'd expect from the neurotypical.

♦♦♦

It's inappropriate to make a "dad joke" if you are not a dad. It's a faux pa.

Great, now we're targeting women, especially women unable to have children. You make me sick.

♦♦♦

Did you hear about the two thieves who stole a calendar? They each got six months.

That's because they were white. If they were People of Color they would have gotten life sentences.

♦♦♦

I'm terrified of elevators so I'm going to start taking

steps to avoid them.

Yeah, you know what? Go ahead and make fun of people with claustrophobia. Any problem you don't have is a punchline, right? Ugh, disgusting.

◆◆◆

A friend of mine didn't pay his exorcist. He got repossessed.

Did he also get decades of therapy to fix what his priest did to him when he was a child? A CHILD. But sure, let's all have a laugh.

◆◆◆

There's no hole in your shoe? Then how'd you get your foot in it?

This is really classist and insensitive. Not everyone can afford new shoes every time they need them.

◆◆◆

When the two rabbit ears got married, it was a nice ceremony. But the reception was amazing.

This literally makes no sense. Whatever.

EPILOGUE

Judgement's not tomorrow
It's today, it's now, it's here
But no it isn't Jesus
Take a look at all your peers
They're all looking down on you
Inside they know what's best for you
EVERYBODY KNOWS WHAT'S BEST FOR YOU
EVERYBODY KNOWS WHAT'S BEST FOR YOU ...
-- Bad Religion, "Best for You" (1988)

"The woke ruin everything."
-- Dan Crenshaw, Hold These Truths podcast, Episode 132

If you enjoyed this book, please leave a review. Also, check out my other books:

Woke Fragility: Bringing Moderates to Heel

A parody of Robin DiAngelo's intellectual dirty diaper, "White Fragility."

Scary Stories to Tell the Woke in the Dark

If you enjoyed "Scary Stories to Tell in the Dark" as a kid, you'll love this anthology of short stories written in the same tone.

Finally, if you'd like to know when I publish another book, you can sign up for my mailing list. I have no intention of blathering on, selling your information, or anything else nefarious. You might see one email a month.

www.subscribepage.com/tm

-- *Tired Moderate*

ABOUT THE AUTHOR

The Tired Moderate is tired, and moderate. I mock the radical left because it acts like the radical right, and I don't want to live in a theocracy, even one run by ostensible atheists.

Printed in Great Britain
by Amazon

10585650R00037